# Baby Tips™
## for new moms

# 9 to 12 Months

# Baby Tips™
## *for new moms*

# 9 to 12 Months

FISHER BOOKS

JEANNE MURPHY

Publishers:       Bill Fisher
                  Helen V. Fisher
                  Howard W. Fisher

Managing Editor: Sarah Trotta

Cover Design:     FifthStreet*design*, Berkeley, CA

Production:       Deanie Wood
                  Randy Schultz
                  Josh Young

Cover Illustration: © 1998 Sharon Howard Constant

Illustrations:    Cathie Lowmiller

Published by
Fisher Books
4239 W. Ina Road, Suite 101
Tucson, Arizona 85741
(520) 744-6110

To pass along your own helpful suggestions to
new mothers for future editions of this book,
please call (800) 617-4603.

**Library of Congress Cataloging-in-Publication Data**
Murphy, Jeanne, 1964-
    [Baby tips for new moms, 9 to 12 months]
    Jeanne Murphy's baby tips for new moms,
      9 to 12 months.
        p.   cm.
    Includes index.
    ISBN 1-55561-168-0
    1. Infants. 2. Infants—Care. 3. Infants—
      Development. 4. Mother and infant.
    HQ774.M889 1998
    649'. 122—dc21                         98-16465
                                               CIP

*Notice:* The information in this book is true and complete to the best of our knowledge. It is
offered with no guarantees on the part of the author or Fisher Books. Author and publisher
disclaim all liability in connection with the use of this book.

The suggestions made in this book are opinions and are not meant to supersede a doctor's
recommendation in any way. Always consult your doctor before beginning any new program.

# Contents

# 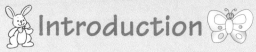 Introduction

You can receive no greater gift than the happiness of being around your children. Babies in the 9- to 12-month age range have learned many basic skills. Now they can concentrate on their true personalities, which emerge like the sun.

Everything is exciting to them, and if it isn't, they will let you know it! Have fun growing with your child and seeing the world through his eyes during this special time, because babies really do see some things more clearly than we do.

*Jeane*

# Ninth Month

Babies love hats! Dress up yourself or the baby—either way, it's good for a few laughs. Collect all the hats you can, from baseball caps to snow hats. (The best part is that later you can use them again by giving them to your husband.)

**H**ugs are one of the best things in life! Hug each member of your family every day. Tell them you love them and how important they are to you . . . especially through their teenage years.

If you find yourself at the doctor's office constantly, perhaps because your baby gets ear infections or sinus problems, ask your doctor to treat your baby with a different medicine.

Often the doctor has several options to choose from, so if one medicine isn't working, you can try another. Your baby

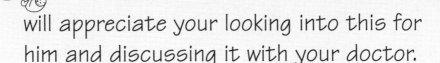

will appreciate your looking into this for him and discussing it with your doctor.

Bear in mind that, although the file in the doctor's office may contain almost a year's worth of information, **you** are the one in charge of noticing repeat occurrences and reporting them—**not the other way around.**

**D**on't keep medications or vitamins in your purse or handbag, even if the containers have childproof caps. Children love to play with Mom's things. A purse is one of the most attractive things they can put their hands on.

Use the weekly grocery-store or toy-store circular as a learning tool! Your child will love picking out the items he uses and sees so often at home with you. It's like getting a new book every week in the mail.

Make sure your baby sees the ocean and touches the sand whenever possible.

If you live far from an ocean, let your child touch the bark of a 100-year-old tree and roll in the grass every sunny day.

If you live in the city, no problem! My boys would trade anything to live in a place with so many wheels and trains. My niece would also pay a pretty price to live in an area where she could admire bridal gowns on display and other window-shopping delights.

The object is to make wherever you live fun (reading books about your area helps)!

**S**ome babies love older folks, so visit older relatives or stop by a nursing home—it will brighten **everyone's** day. Your visit also provides a good opportunity to teach your children to treat older adults with respect.

Save yourself a lot of aggravation and keep a set of diapers, wipes and blankets on each level or area of your house.

Don't wait to instill a love for home in your child. Make family recipes such as "Grandma's secret spaghetti sauce," "Mom's cinnamon rolls," "Dad's pancakes" and "roasted chicken on Sundays." You will be glad you did! Long after they've grown up, your children will come home because they want to taste mom's (and dad's) home-cooked meals again.

(Strange fact: Even if they don't eat these family foods right now, they will still learn to love them by smelling them!)

The Fourth of July will be lots of fun starting at age three or so, but for now expect the loud firecrackers to bother your baby and make her scream.

Instead of talking to yourself, tell your child everything you are thinking. Give him descriptive words so he can increase his vocabulary.

Plan a one-day vacation for you and your husband at home. Find a friend and tell her you will gladly reciprocate (someday) but you would like her to baby-sit for the day and evening—at her house. You can go out to lunch or dinner with your husband, clean the house for once, take a nap, stay up late to watch a movie, or just stay home alone and then sleep in.

Start now to teach your child to leave other people's knickknacks alone when visiting their house. Watch him carefully and remind him as needed until this idea is ingrained in his head: **You can't play with everything everywhere you go!**

If your baby is a picky eater, take him out to the food court of your local mall. Seat him next to the salad bar, pasta station or pizza parlor and aim his chair at another baby his age or slightly older who likes what he is eating.

Your baby loves to learn new tricks to show off, and if you buy him the **same food** . . . you will probably see a new side of your baby.

**T**each your child to sing by singing to him!

Applaud every time your baby stops what she is doing, looks at you and smiles. At that moment, she feels as though she has accomplished something—maybe she pulled herself up to stand and then let go and dropped back to the floor.

She is getting ready to take her first steps, and she needs your support! It's a little scary for her—how would you feel about trying a back-handspring right now for the first time?

If you instill a love of reading, puzzles, crayons and painting (with water) early, you will be able to keep your child occupied for hours between the ages of one and five.

Put on some music and watch your child get into the rhythm. Who said you had to **learn** to dance?

Always empty water pails as soon as you are done with them. Babies can easily fall into water pails.

Toilet bowls are a hazard too. To protect against drowning, use a toilet-lid lock and keep bathroom doors closed at all times.

Use safety gates, but not the accordian-fold type or the kind used to contain pets.

Bring along the gate when you visit others' homes. If they don't have one and your baby can crawl, your visit will only last about 5 minutes.

If you can't build a snowman, bake one! Use a sugar-cookie recipe and your imagination and you're on your way.

Baby Tips

If you have a porch, check to be sure it is enclosed by vertical spindles no more than four inches apart. A baby may get caught in—or fall through—anything wider. Don't take a chance!

Every morning and afternoon, at a window facing the street, let your child watch the other youngsters in the neighborhood get on and off the school bus or walk to and from school.

Baby Tips

Choose a specific time every day to sit down together and read a book instead of watching TV.

It's likely your child will love to eat meat. Make sure you feed her foods from the other food groups first, such as fruits, vegetables, breads and cereals. Introduce meats last.

Children this age bite everything—but they shouldn't bite **everyone.** If your baby bites others, call your doctor right away and take steps to stop this behavior.

Biting jeopardizes the welfare of both children and is never acceptable.

If your child squints, have her eyes checked. If she only reacts to the TV if the volume is high, have her ears checked.

Testing babies is difficult; it's probably best to assume results are questionable to the age of four, when children are easier to test. If you are suspicious about the results or notice ongoing symptoms, get a second opinion.

If you are planning to see Santa this Christmas and your child is less than two years old, expect him to cry and be miserable.

**H**ere's a great toy for under ten dollars: a plastic sprinkler! This toy is terrific because it's fun at any age (your child can play with it too!).

Look for "loopholes" in your baby's pattern—and take advantage of them. For instance, if one night your child is exhausted but awake, put him to sleep without a bottle. If he goes to sleep, try to omit the bottle from the ritual the next night also.

**B**e advised: Older children will attempt to show your baby by example which foods to eat—and which to avoid. Feed your baby separately if you have older children who won't eat what you want to feed your baby.

Teach your child to be positive, not negative. If you need to learn this attitude yourself, rent the movie *Pollyanna*. You'll both be playing the Glad Game in no time!

If you are letting your baby cry in the crib and he is almost quiet, don't let him see you checking on him. The minute he sees you, you'll be back to square one!

Tenth Month

Use the "magic words" around your baby and to your baby at all times. In case you have forgotten, the magic words include: **please, excuse me, thank you** and **you're welcome.**

*G*ive your child the floor and let him show off at least once every day.

If you drop off your child at a daycare center and she throws a fit, don't spend all day feeling guilty. If it's a good daycare center (one you've checked out carefully), your baby will probably stop crying as soon as you're gone. Don't prolong the agony by hanging around. Out of sight, out of mind!

**F**or the next couple of years, expect to have a cranky grouch with you wherever you go. This way, often you will be pleasantly surprised rather than disappointed on your outings. (I'm not talking about your baby.)

No matter what, mother and father must show a united front where baby is concerned.

**D**on't make your child a pizza for dinner when you are serving chicken to the rest of the family—unless you **want** her to expect special foods every night.

Don't let Junior near other children if he's sick or has been sick in the past 24 hours (even if he seems fine). It's not fair to the other children—or their parents!

The sounds of an ambulance, fire truck and police car take on new meaning once you are a parent, don't they?

If your child won't eat dinner at the table, try using a candle as a center-piece and watch what happens!

Flickering candles mesmerize babies as much as they do adults. Just make certain to keep the candle flame far from baby, don't use a tablecloth, and hide all matchbooks.

By now, you may be able to tell if your child has a fever just by holding her next to you. If your baby feels different, especially if she feels hot, use a thermometer to see if she has a temperature.

If your child is wound up and imitates the Tasmanian Devil, try removing all sugar from his diet before you have him examined for attention deficit disorder (ADD).

Some juices have lots of sugar, so avoid them. Watch liquids such as iced tea, apple juice and powdered drinks, too.

**M**ake sure your child doesn't play baseball with the potatoes, put carrots in the toilet or broccoli in your drink—at least while your friends are over.

If you haven't done it already, install safety latches on cabinets, in the pantry and on the oven and refrigerator doors.

Children go through "growth spurts" for years. If your child normally picks at food and suddenly she is asking for seconds at every meal, get ready to go shopping! She is probably getting ready to grow again.

Youngsters love to hear stories. It doesn't matter what the story is about. If you don't know a story, no problem—make one up!

(That's what a story is.)

$G$ive your baby a lollipop, pacifier or bottle just before takeoff on an airplane. This will get him to swallow and relieve the pressure in his ears.

Take time to explain to your child how streams run into rivers and rivers run into oceans. Children's book *Paddle-to-the-Sea*, by Holling Clancy Holling, tells this story from the perspective of a toy canoe that floats from the Great Lakes to the Atlantic Ocean.

Babies absorb everything you say. Even if you don't think they're listening, it's sinking in.

**D**on't ever laugh at your child's bad habits. Stop them right away!

For instance, if your baby tries to get his way by throwing a temper tantrum, take away the toy he's playing with or adjust the situation so you're in control. He will learn what you say, goes. The longer you wait, the harder it will be to change his behavior.

$O$nce your baby starts dropping toys outside the playpen and hurling stuffed animals over the side of the crib, I suspect she is thinking, "You first—I'm right behind you!"

If you hear a loud thump on the monitor, check it out fast. Your baby may have decided the risk was worth the reward and climbed out of her crib.

Teach your child how to visit friends and spend the night at another person's house early in life. This will prevent a lot of midnight pickups and interrupted date nights for you later on.

Babies are curious at this age. They will find scissors, poison **and anything else you don't want them to have**. Put dangerous substances (including furniture polishes) and tools well out of reach or in a locked cabinet **now**. Don't wait!

$S$ometimes your baby will be so tired that you'll have to close his eyes for him.

Have fun and establish private jokes with your child. For instance, your baby may smile every time you wink your eye, raise your eyebrow or make biting noises with your teeth. You can use these special signals to entertain your child when she is cranky and you are stuck somewhere without a toy (a line at the grocery store, in the car waiting to pick up Dad).

**W**hen your child shows you his "boo-boo," he is baring his soul. Always acknowledge him.

Parents are subjective when it comes to their child, no matter how hard they try not to be. And this is wonderful. Always stick up for your child unless you know they are in the wrong.

Make eating fun! For instance, when introducing vegetables to your baby, divide them among the separate compartments of a cupcake pan. Not only will your child learn to distinguish one vegetable from another, but it will help you learn which ones he likes best!

Someone said, "It's OK to lose a battle here and there as long as you win the war." I am certain this statement was coined by a parent.

Baby Tips

Kids grow faster during the summer!

Babies don't know how to hide their emotions . . . and most parents don't know how to show their emotions.

$E$ach child has her own spirit. Enjoy your child's and do everything you can to protect and encourage it.

Let your child get dirty! Make sure he has plenty of play clothes, and I mean **play** clothes—the kind that can get dirty, torn and tossed, if need be.

As scary as it may seem, your child imitates you in every way. If you have a bratty, bossy or "snotty" child, often the best thing to do is look in the mirror and change yourself.

Don't forget to notice the wind! Watching the shaking branches of a tree is fun, and who knows, maybe the tree is trying to wave hello to us. Noticing the wind is the perfect way to encourage your child to use his imagination.

Teach your child to follow directions early. Being able to follow directions is an important skill for such things as cleaning up—and school!

And yes, encourage assertiveness, but don't allow your child to dictate directions to others. After all, he's no expert—he has a lot to learn about life yet!

Empty, open-ended boxes make great tunnels.

# Eleventh Month

As your child learns to talk, you will become a good translator. Notice that phrases such as, "Please, Mom, please!" mean he knows he shouldn't have whatever it is he is asking for.

If you truly want to keep your baby occupied in a playpen, forget toys! Instead, give him the things you use all day—pots, pans, spoons, strainers and toothbrushes are all well-loved by little ones.

 uy any fort, doll house or riding toy
you find on sale. Children this age play
without regard to gender.

Baby Tips

Freeze a loaf of sliced bread. Then use your favorite cookie cutters to make small sandwich shapes from the slices. Get out the peanut butter and jelly and you're set for a tea party! (Add a little colored sugar on top of each "tea sandwich" for real excitement.)

For "tea," serve lemonade (actually diluted lemon water): One lemon wedge squeezed into 8 to 10 ounces of water.

If you are going somewhere quiet, such as a library or a place of worship, make sure to bring along a pacifier or something your child can suck on. As your child gets older, add a lollipop or fruit-leather snack. Those really keep little mouths busy!

Try to break baby's bad habits while you're in a new environment. For example, "lose" a bottle or a pacifier while you are on vacation. In new surroundings, baby may become preoccupied and forget that item more easily than she would at home.

Do you have a child-size slide in your yard? Clean it off and bring it into your baby's room for the winter months. It is also a great idea to bring a slide into the house during nighttime gatherings to give the kids something special to do.

If your baby doesn't like a lot of foods, try to figure out if it is only "messy" foods—like soups or mashed pota-toes—that distress him. Sometimes babies who also fuss over their dirty hands and face find soft foods less appealing.

You can find out by substituting a new texture, such as dry toast, for the "messy" ones when he's upset.

If you or your husband are in the grocery store and you forgot your shopping list, just buy bread, formula, diapers and pizza.

Babies are not allowed to be born unless they like pizza.

$B$elieve it or not, you have to grow a child. They need sunlight, fresh air and lots of water.

If your baby-sitter hangs around to visit with the family after she's been paid, consider adopting her!

I read my baby's horoscope recently and it said, "Enjoy spending quality time at home. You have been on the go for so long now that you need to learn how to relax. Good news! A roadblock in your way has graciously been removed." It was funny, because the day before, I had taken down the child's gate between the family room and the kitchen . . .

Mom needs rest every day, just like baby. If you can, try to slip in a nap somewhere. It really makes a difference and you will feel great!

Make a commitment to be a good parent. You can never love too much.

$S$pend time with your baby and say "I love you" as many times a day as you can.

**V**eteran mothers have learned that you check on babies when you **don't** hear them, less often when you **do**.

If your child is attached to a special toy or stuffed animal, try to get your hands on an exact duplicate, and **never** let the second one out of the house!

If you forget the original at a friend's house, lose it or it wears out, you'll have "old reliable" to pull out and save the day . . . or night, if the special "toy" happens to be a blanket.

If your child indicates he actually **wants** to take medicine, move all of it to another place and double-lock the cupboard doors. This includes vitamins and the aspirin or other medications you might carry in your purse.

As your baby grows, the best way to teach him to blow his nose is to cover his mouth for short intervals.

If your child is quiet, she is probably getting into something.

Little Tykes® toys sell out at garage sales by 8:00 a.m. Shop early!

Forget exercise. To avoid a heart attack, keep all peanuts, popcorn, caramels and hard candy out of the house. They are choking hazards and babies **will** find them.

Don't allow these foods, or hot dogs, until your baby is well over three years old.

$S$ometimes you just have to fake out your children. For example, if you want them to sit by the window, put them by the door instead. They will head for the window automatically!

Baby Tips

**B**ugs amaze children. Never kill one in front of a child. Instead, gently move it outside in a paper towel or cup so it can "go home to its family."

By now or very shortly, your child is walking about and will have full reign of the house. Make sure to teach your little one to eat only at the table, because it will save you many hours of cleanup later.

**T**rade-in or sell your maternity
and outgrown baby clothes at
a used-clothing shop.

If you are planning a garage sale, send the baby away for the day. If the baby stays, he will cry whenever someone buys something and tries to leave with it . . . and you will have to put everything back in the garage at the end of the day.

Baby Tips

$E$very now and then my grandmother used to tell me, "I made you eggs, oatmeal with sugar and toast with butter for breakfast." Then she would give me an oatmeal cookie!

Remember the poor man's medicine and give your child lots of water.

**F**orgive yourself if you make a mistake or lose your patience.

Take your child to an aquarium—a swimming fish with puckering lips elicits gales of giggles at this age.

# Twelfth Month

Save yourself a lot of money on your baby's upcoming 1-year birthday party and just wrap a couple of empty boxes. Tearing off the paper will be your baby's favorite part of the day, anyway!

Infants are born secure and then develop insecurities. Say "You are not allowed to because I said so," and "That is too dangerous to play with," instead of "You can't do that."

Some children want to hold books and look at the pictures just because they see their parents reading. This is the most wonderful kind of patterning!

Baby Tips

Don't spend a fortune on favors for your 1-year-old's birthday party. The only favor your little guests need is the party, believe me.

Don't forget the chicken soup if your child is sick. Thicken soup by adding broken crackers to the broth.

If your baby slips and falls on his bottom in the bathtub, help him immediately, but calmly. Make him feel as though he helped himself. You will help your child build self-confidence and a sense of security. You will teach him to handle these startling situations without panicking.

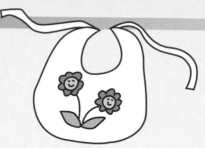

Does your child eat **lots** of blueberries? Then don't be surprised to find his diaper has turned blue. (Red juices have a similar effect.) This can be a scary discovery, but don't worry. What goes in must come out!

**B**uild a tradition with your child. For instance, my mother gives my children and their cousins the same Easter bunny every year to play with for a week. You should see their faces light up when they see their old friend!

For the next couple of years, your child will be learning to talk, but he will only tell the truth. Children do not learn to lie until much later. If you hear a child make observations such as "you're fat" . . . well, maybe your child is gifted.

*G*et together with your friends and swap your children's toys now and then. To a child, no toy is better than someone else's.

Always buy the same food for every child in the car, and buy the same toy for every child in the room from now on.

If you are planning a big birthday bash for your 1 year old, and you expect all your friends and their babies to attend, plan to end the party by 7 p.m.

*O*nce your child learns to say, "But I'm not tired," say, "What does that have to do with anything? Good night!"

Baby Tips

$B$eing around a child has many advantages. One is that you will receive a totally objective opinion in every situation.

**E**xplore the outdoors with your child. The first time your child sees a bird, butterfly, puddle, a dog or a cat may be the first time you've really **seen** one too.

If your child doesn't eat well, try playing a game with her. I like the "beep" game. Say "beep" and when your baby smiles, try to have her take her first bite. Then only say "beep" after she takes another bite. Babies at this age love games like this, and they figure them out easily.

Sometimes you have to break the rules and use the philosophy "as long as they eat." This is especially true if your children are sick. Just getting them to eat **something** is a triumph for both of you. Don't forget ice pops are great for fluids, and kids love them.

Don't plan to give your child his first piece of birthday cake on his actual birthday. He could get sick and he probably won't like it. Instead, try giving it to the baby one week earlier and get him used to it. By the time his party rolls around, he will really enjoy a little birthday cake.

**S**omeone said, "There is no love without discipline, and there is no discipline without love," and I agree completely.

Baby Tips

$O$nce your baby tastes a lollipop, he'll never see another one without wanting it. Immediately.

Make sure to give your child the right toy at the right age. Toys and games usually have age-specific labels. Following the label is a good idea for a couple of reasons.

1. You can be sure the toy doesn't have small pieces that might choke a small child—a major concern.

2. You'll be sure the child is old enough to use the toy for its intended purpose. A child who receives a toy that is too "old" for her won't be able to play the game the way it is meant to be played. She will remember it as a frustrating experience and probably will never like it, even when she is older.

If your child has a stomach virus, stick to fluids like flat ginger ale and white grape juice, in case she needs to vomit. I can say from experience that crib sheets and walls will be ruined if your child drinks anything red, orange or purple.

As your child grows, look for opportunities to help him learn. For example, if you ask your son to hand you the silverware and he just stares at you, ask for forks and spoons instead. Children's vocabularies are only as broad as you make them.

I don't know the medical terminology for this, but essentially what happens is that you have a baby and she gets your memory.

Be on the lookout for buried treasures around your house. Missing any sparkly jewelry or keys? Rest assured baby has them stashed in a special hiding place . . . maybe even in the zippered pouch of a stuffed animal. Don't panic! Because your baby can't tell you where the object is, just put out something else he'll covet. Then sit back and wait. When he goes to hide the second item, he'll lead you to the first one.

**C**ongratulations, Mom and Dad! I am sure you have a very happy 1 year old. Enjoy your baby and his or her celebration!

# Index

## Have a great tip?
### Enter the Baby Tips™ Contest.
## Win more than $5,000 for your baby's education!

Share your special tip to soothe a cranky child, introduce her to the joys of spinach, or prepare him for a potty-training marathon. Come up with the first-prize-winning tip and receive a $5,000.00 educational bond plus hundreds of dollars' worth of baby accessories. Second- and third-place winners will receive an assortment of baby supplies.

Entries must be in the form of a "tip" or suggestion for parents with children age three or younger. Clearly print or type each suggested tip (no more than 75 words) on a 3 x 5 index card. Include your name, address, and daytime phone number. Only one entry per household, but each entry can include several tips.

The Baby Tips™ contest runs September 1, 1998, through January 31, 1999. The winner will be announced in March, 1999. All entries must be original tips created by the contestant. Purchase is not required. Entries will be judged by Fisher Books. All entries and their use become the property of Fisher Books.

Mail your entry to: Baby Tips™ Contest
4239 W. Ina Road #101
Tucson, AZ 85741

# Toys and Activities for Young Children:

**From birth to 3 months,** children begin to smile at people and follow moving persons or objects with their eyes, they prefer faces and bright colors and will turn their head toward sounds.

To engage them in activities, they enjoy: rattles, large rings, squeeze or sucking toys, lullabies, bright pictures of faces, cardboard or vinyl books with high-contrast illustrations.

**From 4 to 6 months,** children prefer parents and older siblings to other people, will repeat actions that have interesting results, laugh, gurgle and imitate sounds.

They enjoy playing with soft dolls, socks with bright designs, toys that make noise when batted, squeezed or mouthed; fingerplays, simple songs and peek-a-boo.

**From 7 to 12 months,** they begin to explore, bang or shake objects with hands, identify themselves, body parts and voices of familiar people. They may become shy or upset with strangers.

They enjoy playing with wooden or soft plastic toy vehicles, large plastic balls, water toys that float, board books to read, puppets and tearing up old magazines.

Reprinted with permission from the brochure *TOYS: Tools for Learning,* available from the National Association for the Education of Young Children.

# Resources for Parents

**Asthma and Allergy Foundation**
Consumer Information Line
1125 15th St. NW, Suite 502
Washington, DC 20005
800-7-ASTHMA
www.aafa.org
Provides information to parents of children
with asthma, reactive airway disease
or allergies.

---

**American Academy of Pediatrics**
141 Northwest Point Blvd.
Elk Grove Village, IL 60009-0927
847-228-5005
www.aap.org
Provides information and publishes free
brochures on children's health issues.

---

**Cesarean Support, Education, and Concern**
22 Forest Rd.
Framingham, MA 01701
508-877-8266
Call to receive local listings of Cesarean
support groups in your area.

**International Parents Without Partners**
800-637-7974
Offers education and referral services.
Organizes events for single parents.

---

**La Leche League Hotline**
800-LALECHE
847-519-7730
www.lalecheleague.org

Provides information and support to nursing
mothers.

---

**National Association for the Education
of Young Children**
1509 16th Street NW
Washington, DC 20036-1426
800-424-2460
www.naeyc.org

Call for brochures and catalog on
other areas of child development
and education.

**National Association of Mothers Centers**
64 Division Avenue
Levittown, NY 11756
800-645-3828
A national network of support and resource
groups for mothers. Contact them to
find your local support center for new
parents—or help you start your own.

---

**National Safe Kids Campaign**
1301 Pennsylvania Ave. NW, Suite 1000
Washington, DC 20004
202-662-0600
www.safekids.org
Offers printed information
on child safety,
including fire safety
and burn prevention.
Seeks to raise public
awareness of child injury prevention.

**Nursing Mothers Counsel, Inc.**
PO Box 500063
Palo Alto, CA 94303
408-272-1448
www.nursingmothers.org
Provides information and support to nursing
mothers.

---

**Postpartum Support, International**
927 North Kellogg Ave.
Santa Barbara, CA 93111
805-967-7636
www.iup.edu/an/postpartum
Email: thonikman@compuserve.com
International network of concerned
individuals and groups dedicated to
increasing awareness about the emotional
health of pregnant and postpartum women
and their families.

---

**US Consumer Product Safety Commission**
Washington, DC 20207
800-638-2772

# CareGuide – The Online Resource for Finding Childcare

Your childcare solution is only a click away!

CareGuide is an easy to use, interactive reference guide of childcare, preschools and day-care providers nationwide. To use, simply follow three steps: Go online to www.careguide.net, click on the "Search for Child Care" button and select your search criteria, then review the list of providers that match your needs. The comprehensive CareGuide listing contains facility-specific information such as: hours of operation, staff-to-child ratio, admission requirements, staff tenure and activities.

With this offer, an experienced CareGuide Referral Specialist will assist you in finding care FREE OF CHARGE. To contact a Referral Specialist, either fill out the form on our home site at www.careguide.net or call toll-free 1-888-389-8839.

Contact Information:
Web site address:   www.careguide.net
E-mail address:     care@careguide.net
Toll-Free Phone:    1-888-389-8839

# PERFECTLY SAFE CATALOG

Keeping children safe is always a major concern for parents. With products from the Perfectly Safe catalog, every room in your home can be made safe. In addition, this catalog provides other useful products for traveling, on-the-go, in the car, and when your child is playing outdoors.

Whether you are looking for a bicycle helmet, a jogging stroller, a sinkadink (a small sink that fits over any standard bathtub) or a device to keep little ones from inserting their grilled cheese sandwich into your VCR, the Perfectly Safe catalog has what you need.

All Perfectly Safe products are tested and approved by families like yours.

To receive your free catalog, call 1-800-837-KIDS from anywhere in the US or Canada, or write:

The Perfectly Safe Catalog
7835 Freedom Ave. NW, Suite 3
North Canton, OH  44720-6907

PFIS98

# Natural Baby Catalog

For the best in all-natural fabrics and materials, child-tested and parent-approved products, look into the Natural Baby Catalog. Specializing in products that emphasize health or comfort, this catalog offers everything from clothing to crib shoes, mocs to natural wooden toys, slides, rocking horses, cotton diapers and much more.

Many products are made of organically grown materials, and many of the companies are home businesses.

To receive a free copy of The Natural Baby Catalog, call 1-800-388-BABY, or write:

Natural Baby Catalog
7835 Freedom Ave. NW, Suite 2
North Canton, OH 44720-6907

NFIS98

# Jeannie's Kid's Club

Want to save money while getting sensible products that will stimulate your child's imagination? Join Jeannie's Kid's Club and save hundreds of dollars on items for the nursery, toys for infants and toddlers, kids furniture and many other products.

If you join Jeannie's Kid's Club you can save up to 40% or more on many items, such as the Bedside Co-sleeper™, a clothing personalizer, pre- & post-natal stretch sleep bras, Comfort Temp™ thermometer, toys and much, much more.

Enjoy a 3-month trial membership for only $3.00!

Call 1-800-363-0500 to find out about Jeannie's Kid's Club, or write:

Kid's Club
7835 Freedom Ave NW, Suite 3
North Canton, OH 44720-6907

KFIS98

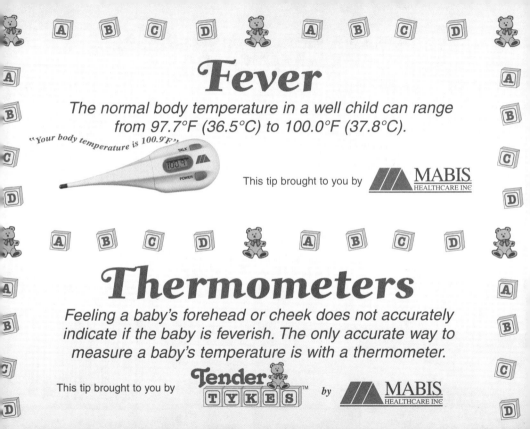

# Fever

*The normal body temperature in a well child can range from 97.7°F (36.5°C) to 100.0°F (37.8°C).*

"Your body temperature is 100.9°F"

This tip brought to you by **MABIS** HEALTHCARE INC

# Thermometers

*Feeling a baby's forehead or cheek does not accurately indicate if the baby is feverish. The only accurate way to measure a baby's temperature is with a thermometer.*

This tip brought to you by **Tender TYKES™** *by* **MABIS** HEALTHCARE INC

**SEARS** Portrait Studio

# Choose the Offer That's Right for You!

---

## 40% OFF Portrait Sheets

**Unlimited Portrait Sheets** $5^{95}$ (Reg. $10)

Plus, Get An Instant Color Proof Sheet & A

# FREE Key Ring*

6 poses taken, choose from over 20 backgrounds & props!

**$13.95 session fee not included in portrait sheet purchase.** Limit one special offer per session. Sheet purchase required for free items. Offer void where prohibited. Cash value 1/20¢. Cannot be combined with other offers. Sears Card and major credit cards accepted. Coupon good through April 3, 1999.
*while supplies last

Appointments accepted. Walk-ins welcome.

**SEARS** Portrait Studio

00000 30053

PRESENT COUPON AT TIME OF SESSION

---

## 50 Portraits

Only $5^{95}$

2-10x13s, 2-8x10s, 2-5x7s, 4-3½x5s and 40 wallets
Plus, Get A

# FREE Key Ring*

**Sitting fee of $8.95 per person,** not included in advertised price. Sitting fee payable when portraits are taken. Portrait package made from first accepted pose. Package purchase required for free item. Three poses taken. Limit one special offer per subject(s). No limit on number of offers per family. Cannot be combined with other offers. Offer void where prohibited. Cash value 1/20¢. Sears Card and major credit cards accepted. Coupon good through April 3, 1999. (90)
*while supplies last

Appointments accepted. Walk-ins welcome.

**SEARS** Portrait Studio

00000 30054

PRESENT COUPON AT TIME OF SITTING

# $5 REBATE ON AN OPTIONS™ OR RISE & DINE® HIGH CHAIR

**To receive your $5 rebate, follow these steps:**

- Buy any Cosco Options or Rise & Dine High Chair and cut out the UPC (bar code symbol) from the carton.
- Mail this form, the UPC and your original dated sales receipt to:

**Cosco Promotion Fulfillment Dept. 069
P.O. Box 2609, Columbus, IN 47202-2609 USA**

Name_____

Address_____

City_____ State_____

Zip_____ Tel ( ) _____

**Rebate requests must be postmarked by December 31, 2000.** Please allow 4 to 6 weeks for receipt of rebate. Limit of one rebate per purchase. Cannot be combined with any other Cosco offer. Must be accompanied by original claim form and sales receipt (facsimiles will not be accepted). Void where prohibited.

# $5 REBATE ON TOURIVA®, REGAL RIDE® OR OLYMPIAN™ CONVERTIBLE CAR SEAT

**To receive your $5 rebate, follow these steps:**

- Buy any Cosco Touriva, Regal Ride or Olympian Car Seat and cut out the UPC (bar code symbol) from the carton.
- Mail this form, the UPC and your original dated sales receipt to:

**Cosco Promotion Fulfillment Dept. 069
P.O. Box 2609, Columbus, IN 47202-2609 USA**

Name_____

Address_____

City_____ State_____

Zip_____ Tel ( ) _____

**Rebate requests must be postmarked by December 31, 2000.** Please allow 4 to 6 weeks for receipt of rebate. Limit of one rebate per purchase. Cannot be combined with any other Cosco offer. Must be accompanied by original claim form and sales receipt (facsimiles will not be accepted). Void where prohibited.